THE COMPLI
LADY ERA

The Step by Step for Effective Treatment of Treatment of Female Sexual Dysfunction, Increase Female Libido and Skyrocket Female Orgasm

ISBN 978-1-7948-0861-4

Halland Nancy

Copyright@2022

TABLE OF CONTENT

CHAPTER 1 3
   INTRODUCTION 3
CHAPTER 2 6
   What is female Viagra (Lady-Era) and how does it work? 6
CHAPTER 3 12
   What types of sexual difficulties does Female Viagra help with? 12
CHAPTER 4 16
   The Advantages of Female Viagra 16
CHAPTER 5 22
   DOES LADY VIAGRA ACTUALLY WORK? 22
CHAPTER 6 33
   SUMMARY OF LADY ERA 33
THE END 41

CHAPTER 1

INTRODUCTION

In accordance with statistics, women are more likely than males to suffer from sexual drive disorders. The majority of the time, the cause is a lack of sexual desire as a result of a low libido.

According to WebMD, around 40% of women, to a greater or lesser extent, suffer from sexual desire problem, also known as female sexual dysfunction in medical terms, according to WebMD. Women's reproductive health is inversely proportional to the level of satisfaction they obtain from intimacy (visit WebMD for more information on this).

The majority of women experience hypoactive sexual desire as a result of psychological factors such as depression, anxiety disorders, chronic stress, emotional strain, and other such factors — all of which are common suspects in female sexual dysfunction.

At times, the psychological factors that contribute to decreased sexual drive are linked to physiologic illnesses, including hormone problems, adverse effects from the use of antidepressants and tranquilizers, alcoholism, obesity (including postpartum changes), and menopause.

Females who have low sex drive have difficulty obtaining fulfillment and orgasm during intimate encounters with their male partners. Ultimately, it might result in bad effects for both spouses.

Females may suffer discomfort during the sexual encounter as well as a lack of willingness to engage in oral sex as a result of the general lack of sex pleasure. They may also be unable to be aroused, and all of these unpleasant consequences are associated with low libido.

Until around ten years ago, the only type of treatment available to such ladies was psychological. Women's major tool in the fight against sexual dysfunction is now Viagra, which is available over the counter.

To date, a number of attempts have been made to resolve female sexual problems with the assistance of antidepressants such as Addyi prescription medication, which, according to Mayo Clinic research, increases sexual response and satisfaction while also causing severe side effects such as fainting as a result of the drug's administration.

CHAPTER 2

What is female Viagra (Lady-Era) and how does it work?

Developed to assist female patients in overcoming sexual difficulties and increasing the joy they obtain from sexual activities, generic Lady Era medicine is now available. Men and women refer to the Era pill as Viagra for women since it is a cutting-edge medical treatment that was developed to help women get more out of their sexual encounters by increasing their sexual arousal and getting more pleasure from their sexual encounters.

For the time being, scientists have been able to tailor the beneficial therapeutic characteristics of Sildenafil to the specific challenges that women face. Sildenafil for women has the same chemical structure as male Viagra, and it operates in a similar manner to Viagra in terms of mechanism of action. However, it is only effective in women, and it enables them to improve their sensitivity to sexual stimulation.

Although not everyone is aware of what Female Viagra is, those who have experienced the beneficial benefits of Lady Era continue to purchase it on a regular basis. What is the point of purchasing Lady Era? Despite the fact that this medication has just recently been introduced to the pharmaceutical market, there is little information available about it, even in expert medical sources.

In today's market, generic sildenafil for women is available under a variety of distinct trade names. Search engines are inundated with questions concerning Lady Era pills, including where to get Generic Femalegra, Lovegra, Womenra, Female Viagra, and other similar products.

Despite the fact that all of these medications have a similar mechanism of action and include sildenafil, they are offered on the market under distinct brand names. Although it appears that one may get Lady Era online under a variety of aliases, the genuine, high-quality tablet is manufactured by Ajanta Pharma. As a result, use caution while purchasing Lady Era tablets and ensure that the manufacturer is identified.

Where can I get Lady Era? The medicine is not available for purchase in physical pharmacies, but it may be purchased online from reputable drugstores that carry the product made by the licensed pharmaceutical business.

Indications and benefits of using Viagra for women

The introduction of Lady Era, generic femalegra, and other similar medications was a watershed moment in medical history, enabling millions of women to shift their perspectives on sexuality.

Women over the age of 50 who have never been satisfied during intimacy may be able to learn to know their own bodies in a new manner, open up new erogen zones, and have high-quality sexual encounters for the first time.

The usage of Lady Era is associated with sexual dysfunction.

Enhances the sensitivity of the erogenic zones in the body.

Increases the amount of intimate lubrication that is produced.

Increases the likelihood of experiencing several orgasms.

It alleviates unpleasant feelings that occur during sexual contact.

The ability of nerve endings in both exterior and internal sexual organs to transmit electricity is improved.

Enhances one's urge to have sexual relations.

The symptoms of frigidity are eliminated with this treatment.

Stress is relieved, the mood is improved, and the hormone balance is maintained.

Immediately after taking the Lade Era pill, women will notice alterations in their appearance and behavior. And, despite the fact that Viagra for women is not a cure-all for sexual dysfunction, this medication will improve the quality of life for any woman who takes it.

CHAPTER 3

What types of sexual difficulties does Female Viagra help with?

According to the data, women are more likely than men to be unsatisfied with a sexual encounter afterward. The vast majority of the time, lack of sexual desire and low libido are the root causes of this condition. According to another study, more than 40% of women suffer from libido issues, which are also known as female sexual dysfunction.

A variety of physiological impairments, including but not limited to hormone imbalances and menopause as well as obesity, postpartum changes, and other factors, can result in significant libido loss.

In general, female sexual dysfunction is characterized with difficulties in obtaining an orgasm and feeling satisfied during intimate encounters. Reduced libido can be caused by difficulties with arousal, discomfort during sex, and other unpleasant experiences.

Unfortunately, the present pharmaceutical industry does not have a simple and effective answer for this problem — Lady Era, often known as Female Viagra. The drug, which contains sildenafil citrate as an active ingredient, helps to achieve the greatest possible outcome. Furthermore, female Viagra is accessible over-the-counter and is considered to be safe to use due to the absence of contraindications.

Viagra For Women is a prescription medication that is used to treat female sexual dysfunction.

Female Viagra is a medication that is used in the treatment of female sexual dysfunctions, particularly in the absence of sexual arousal and a poor reaction to physical sexual stimulation. However, these are not the only ailments that this medication may be able to heal in females. Female Viagra can assist them in getting rid of the following conditions:

Unavailability of lubricant in intimate areas;

During sex, you may experience pain and discomfort.

The incapability of building up to a climax;

Insufficiency of sensibility in intimate zones;

a lack of sex desire;

Relationship issues arising from the misaligned levels of sexual desire in a marriage.

CHAPTER 4

The Advantages of Female Viagra

Originally, Viagra was thought to be a male-only therapy, but Lady Era is a new prescription that has been developed specifically for women who want to increase sexual arousal while also receiving the greatest amount of satisfaction and pleasure during the intercourse. Because of their comparable chemical composition, female Viagra functions in the same way as male Viagra. When it comes to women, however, Viagra's effects are geared at those with advanced sensitivity. In addition, the therapy may be used to:

Erogenic zones will become more sensitive as time goes on.

Increase the amount of vaginal secretion produced;

Reduce the occurrence of uncomfortable sensations during the sexual encounter;

Stress should be reduced, and hormonal imbalances should be reduced.

Reduce the signs of frigidity;

Create a brighter and more accessible environment for orgasms;

restore or rekindle a person's enthusiasm in sexual activity

Enhance your level of enjoyment with your sexual encounters.

Contribute to the improvement of sexual connections within the marriage.

Side effects of Viagra

The greatest time to take Female Viagra is when you are most relaxed.

Take Lady Era one hour before you intend to have sexual relations. During this period, the sildenafil in the Female Viagra formulation will reach its maximal activity in the bloodstream, and the health consequences of the medicine will begin to manifest themselves. You will encounter fewer and milder side effects the longer you use the medication. The better your body responds to it, the better your overall health.

Contraindications or limitations may apply.

If you have any of the following conditions, you should avoid using Female Viagra:

coronary artery disease

Liver disease is a medical condition that affects the liver.

Kidney disease is a medical condition that affects the kidneys.

Degenerative eye illnesses are a group of diseases that affect the eyes' ability to regenerate.

ulcer in the stomach or duodenum

Disorders of the clotting process

disorders of the blood cells

hypertension (high blood pressure) difficulties

during pregnancy or during nursing

What is the impact of female Viagra on male sexual performance?

Female Viagra and the traditional tablet for men both include the same active ingredient, sildenafil citrate, which is the same as in male Viagra. Because this chemical is also used to treat PAH (pulmonary arterial hypertension) in both male and female patients, the usage of Female Viagra is both safe and useful in both genders. The mechanism of action of sildenafil in males, on the other hand, is a little different: it increases erectile hardness and the mechanical capacity to engage in sexual act without impairing desire levels.

After everything is said and done, it can be concluded that, in the absence of contraindications, Lady Era may be used by both couples. However, it is preferable to use items that are particularly created for each partner, and ideally after consulting with a doctor.

CHAPTER 5
DOES LADY VIAGRA ACTUALLY WORK?

In today's society, sexual dysfunctions are highly common and widespread. Stress, a hectic daily schedule, worry, relationship troubles, and other issues commonly lead to a drop in female sexual desire and a decline in male erectile function. The data show that at some time in their lives, more than 40% of the female population will experience reduced libido and diminished sexual desire. Women's sexual dysfunction can be caused by a variety of factors, ranging from psychological and emotional factors to physical factors. It is possible that stress, worry, relationship troubles, low self-esteem, and other comparable feelings will limit the desire to have sexual intercourse. The inability to have orgasm and satisfaction during a sexual encounter is the most common sign of sexual dysfunction. Such a situation has negative effects for both spouses as a result of its existence.

Because of the quick and intensive growth of the pharmaceutical business, people are now able to receive appropriate treatment for even the most uncommon and unique medical disorders that exist. The female version of Viagra is just what you need to overcome the debilitating symptoms of a sex problem and reclaim your ability to have a healthy sexual encounter. Like regular Viagra, this medicine has a profound effect on the body and should not be used lightly. The medicine, which has the same active component, interferes with the functions of the body's organs and processes in a similar manner. The outcomes that are accomplished, on the other hand, will vary, with the most common and promising being as follows:

Increased sexual desire; increased libido; increased sensitivity of erogenous zones;

removal of pain during the intercourse; reduction of indications of frigidity, among other things.

what occurs when a man falls in love with a woman

What Happens When a Woman Uses a Male Viagra Prescription?

Female Viagra is a cutting-edge drug that is gaining widespread acceptance at an alarming rate. Some women, on the other hand, believe that male Viagra is preferable and see no reason to purchase a female version. Despite the fact that this field of pharmacology has not been well investigated, a number of research have revealed that male Viagra does not provide beneficial outcomes in males. Instead, it can cause a variety of unpleasant responses and undesired side effects to occur.

Male Viagra cannot be taken in the same manner that female Viagra cannot be taken by guys. So, if you're still wondering what happens when a guy takes female Viagra, you should have a look at a list of probable adverse effects that can be caused by improper usage of the prescription. Regardless of the numerous reports of beneficial benefits, both male and female Viagra have a comparable, but not identical, impact on the body, which means they should only be used in line with the manufacturer's instructions. To understand more about the safety of female Viagra for males and vice versa, speak with your healthcare professional now.

The proper administration of medications is a guarantee of a successful treatment course with the desired outcomes, whilst the tiniest misapplication of medications can cause a variety of life-threatening health responses and problems. Patients under the age of 18 are not permitted to take either the male or female Viagra.

Female Viagra - Sildenafil Citrate for Females

Female Viagra is a prescription medication.

According to the research Prevalence of Female Sexual Dysfunction, hypoactive sexual drive in women is an issue that affects 40.9 percent of premenopausal women alone. Premenopausal women are more likely than other age groups to have reduced sex drive, as are more female patients in general. The usage of oral tablets has been shown to have a good effect on sexual desire, particularly when used to treat low sexual desire. Sildenafil is effective as a female libido medicine, despite the fact that it was originally intended for usage in males (sildenafil branded as Viagra treats erectile difficulty).

Multiple concerns associated with sexual drive disorder are addressed when female Viagra is taken before to the scheduled sexual activity, according to the manufacturer. No matter what is causing female sexual desire problems in contemporary women, libido drugs increase the intensity of passion and pleasure gained from sex in both men and women who take them. According to reports, 82 percent of women found Viagra to be successful in re-igniting their sexual desire, alleviating coital discomfort, improving vaginal lubrication, and assisting them in achieving orgasmic feelings.

Is There a Brand Name For Female Viagra

While the active ingredient in medications to increase female sexual desire is sildenafil citrate, the brand names of the drugs might differ from one another. Lady Era, Femalegra, and Lovegra are three of the most well-known tablets for increasing female sexual pleasure that are manufactured by the Indian pharmaceutical business Ajanta Pharma Ltd.: Lady Era, Femalegra, and Lovegra. Both of these tablets contain sildenafil 100 mg, with the only difference between them being the trademark name - they are equally effective in combating sexual desire dysfunction.

What is the mechanism of action of Viagra in women?

Viagra for women works by increasing the flow of blood to the genitals, which helps to treat female sexual dysfunction. Because of the dilatation of blood vessels in the vagina, increased blood circulation occurs, which in turn increases the sensitivity of the clitoris and the walls of the vaginal canal. Additionally, Bartholin glands are activated indirectly, which results in improved vaginal lubrication.

As a consequence of the effects of Female Viagra on the body, hypoactive sexual desire symptoms such as vaginal dryness, reduced sensitivity, discomfort during the sexual act, and poor sexual drive are addressed and eradicated, as well as erectile dysfunction.

The following are some of the advantages that may be obtained through the usage of Female Viagra:

Generic viagra tablets are available for purchase online.

A spike in sexual interest in the relationship rekindled sexual desire in both of them.

Extensive, incredibly delightful feelings during penetrative sex, as well as strong orgasms / numerous orgasms, are produced by this product.

intrapersonal connections have been improved

How long does it take for Female Viagra to begin to function effectively?

What is the best way to take the pills for sexual arousal disorder? Taking the tablet with a sufficient amount of water around 60 minutes before sexual activity is the general rule of thumb, followed by waiting for the drug's effects to take effect. The initial indicators of Female Viagra impacting the body are a pleasant feeling of warmth that may begin in the face but will eventually focus on the lower stomach and the vagina, leading in increased sexual desire and arousal. Depending on the dosage, the effects of Female Viagra might last up to 8 hours.

In what ways can Female Viagra have negative effects on the body?

While the sildenafil contained in Female Viagra is intended to alleviate low sexual desire, it may produce other transitory changes in the body, just as any other medication would. Those modifications are referred to as side effects, and they are only temporary.

Many women do not experience them at all, while others encounter relatively minimal side effects, such as those associated with using generic sildenafil.

headache flushing of the face

Inflammation of the stomach and nausea Rhinitis / sinusitis

If the adverse effects do not subside, it is good to consider the possibility of increasing the dose with your doctor.

Female Viagra in Generic Form

Generic medications are manufactured by businesses that were not involved in the development of the original drug. In the case of Female Viagra, there are a variety of generic alternatives that are reasonably priced. They are just as safe and effective as the original medications, but they provide an opportunity to address low sexual desire while saving a significant amount of money.

For female sexual dysfunction, Lovegra, Femalegra, and Lady Era are some of the most effective sildenafil-based medications available today. For example, Cialis For Women (tadalafil) and Vyleesi (bremelanotide) are analogs of Female Viagra that contain other chemicals. These medications all address the problem of female sexual arousal in a different way, and they are all available over the counter. As a result, Female Cialis increases libido in the same way as Female Viagra does by increasing blood flow. In the case of Addyi, it is an antidepressant medication, while in the case of Vyleesi, it is a chemical that is injected into the abdomen prior to participating in sexual activity. It is debated whether the latter two drugs should be used because of the major adverse effects they might induce as well as the extended (Addyi) / unpleasant (Vyleesi) administration.

CHAPTER 6
SUMMARY OF LADY ERA

What exactly is Lady Era?

Lady Era is a prescription medication sold to women that is said to improve poor sex desire. Sildenafil citrate is the primary active component in this product. It is also included in Viagra, which is one of the most often prescribed drugs for the treatment of erectile dysfunction in males.

It is claimed to be an authorized therapy for female sexual dysfunction in various countries, although it is not currently available for purchase in the United Kingdom. It is not currently an authorized treatment since there is insufficient data to demonstrate that it is effective in the treatment of female sexual dysfunction at this time.

Return to the top of the page

Is it possible to purchase Lady Era on the internet?

Lady Era is not available for purchase in the United Kingdom since it has not been licensed for use in the country to treat female sexual dysfunction. Anywhere that sells Lady Era for ladies to persons in the United Kingdom is doing it in violation of the law. Even in other countries, purchasing Lady Era from online merchants includes a certain amount of danger because it is impossible to determine whether the sellers are authentic and which countries Lady Era is legal to purchase in.

Return to the top of the page

Does Lady Era have any effect?

Lady Era is not licensed for use as a pharmaceutical in the United Kingdom, and it has not been shown to be useful in the treatment of female sexual dysfunction. There have been a few studies conducted to investigate the effects of sildenafil, the active component in Lady Era, on female sexual dysfunction. These include the following:

According to the findings of a research on sildenafil and decreased sex desire in women, there was no discernible benefit.

There was some improvement in a smaller study of sildenafil for women who had poor sex drive.

Some evidence suggests that sildenafil might improve vaginal symptoms associated with sex, but not sex drive, in post-menopausal women, according to one research.

A small-scale investigation revealed that sildenafil may be effective in alleviating the sexual function-related adverse effects of SSRIs (antidepressants)

In contrast, another study found that women with type 1 diabetes who took sildenafil saw improvements in sexual function.

Overall, the data is contradictory and does not support the claim that sildenafil is a good treatment for women suffering from sexual dysfunction.

Return to the top of the page

Are there any Lady Era reviews available on the internet?

There are only a few reviews for Lady Era, and they are not trustworthy. The product may be sold illegally on various websites, as evidenced by the fact that some sites provide customer ratings without displaying specific comments from consumers. Because Lady Era has not been demonstrated to work, it is unlikely to receive good feedback.

Return to the top of the page

Is it planned to authorize Lady Era in the United Kingdom?

There are no intentions to approve Lady Era in the United Kingdom since the evidence does not support the use of sildenafil for the treatment of female sexual dysfunction at this time. Products like Lady Era will not be allowed for sale in the United Kingdom until there is sufficient proof that sildenafil is effective in treating female sexual dysfunction.

Return to the top of the page

Is Lady Era in any danger?

A doctor would have to authorize products containing sildenafil for ladies such as Lady Era in order for them to be considered safe for you. Because it is not yet permitted in the United Kingdom, this is unlikely to occur. Even if it were authorized, a complete medical history would need to be obtained before to dispensing to confirm that the medication was safe for the individual to consume.

When used by women, Lady Era has the potential to induce many of the same negative effects as sildenafil medicines do in males. Furthermore, because it is not adequately regulated, it is uncertain whether Lady Era includes what it promises to contain or whether it contains dangerously high doses of prescription medicine.

In an independent investigation conducted by the Therapeutic Goods Administration in Australia, it was discovered that Lady Era includes several substances that have not been reported by the manufacturer. Since Lady Era contains substances that are typically only available through a prescription, it is possible that you are putting your health at risk by using it.

Return to the top of the page

When it comes to treating female sexual dysfunction, what therapy choices are accessible to you?

In the United Kingdom, there are no drugs licensed for the treatment of female sexual dysfunction. However, in the United States, Flibanserin is approved for the treatment of female sexual dysfunction and is marketed under the brand name Addyi. For example, flibanserin, unlike sildenafil (Lady era), is a drug that is used to treat low sex desire in women that is not caused by a pre-existing medical condition, psychological condition, or relationship difficulty. Addyi has not yet been authorized for usage in the United Kingdom.

It is always advisable to exercise caution when ordering drugs online because many internet firms claim to provide 'female viagra,' which often includes the same active component as male Viagra (sildenafil) and has not been proved to aid with female sexual dysfunction. These goods, like Lady Era, may also include other components that have not been disclosed by the product's producers.

A number of herbal products are also available in the United Kingdom that are aimed at enhancing female sexual performance, such as Prelox, which is one example. Nevertheless, because they have not been licensed as drugs and are not adequately controlled, these products are unreliable in the same manner as female Viagras are.

The most effective strategy for women to address their sexual dysfunction is to seek assistance and counseling from a sex therapist.

THE END

Made in the USA
Monee, IL
08 September 2022